Adam SOMETIMES Can't Sit Still

Written By
Jo Oliver-Yeager

Other Books By Jo Oliver-Yeager

Sophie Counts Her Steps

Copyright © 2020 Kind Words Publishing
ISBN 978-1-7358815-1-5

All rights reserved. This book may not be reproduced in whole or in part in any form, or by any means, without express written permission from the publisher.

Published by:

Kind Words Publishing
kindwordspublishing@gmail.com

This is dedicated to all you wonderful and talented people with ADHD. Especially *you* (you know who you are) xoxox

This book is one in a series intended to educate people about acceptance and understanding as well as giving a voice to anyone who may not fit into that "neat little box."

For my wonderful Tony and the inspiration of my three babies who hold my heart- Nyan, Tessa, & Auden for always supporting my love of writing.

"Adam, sit up please," asked Mrs. Roberts, his 3rd grade teacher.

Adam had a hard time sitting still. In fact, Adam got in trouble every hour on the hour at school. Third grade was tough for him.

He wondered why some of his friends could sit and do the work but he couldn't sit still.

One day, the week of his class Halloween party, he decided he would try to sit and pay attention in English class. After all, he liked English. He liked his teacher and he didn't want to let Ms. Monaco down.

Today's book was *James and The Giant Peach* (one of Adam's favorites.) His mom has read it to him since he was little.

Before he realized, he yelled out, "A rhinoceros kills them!" The other classmates all turned to look at Adam. They weren't quite sure what he meant.

Ms. Monaco had not reached the part on how James lost his parents. But Adam was way past where she had started.

"Adam, please raise your hand. We haven't gotten to that part yet," Ms. Monaco said as she went back to explaining what the book was going to be about.

Adam felt bad.

His favorite class. His favorite teacher, and his favorite book and he still managed to get into trouble. He felt upset with himself.

On his bus ride home, Adam didn't recall what happened in English because he got in trouble in ALL of his classes.

While on the bus, he kept switching from his seat to the one next to Sam. Sam kept pushing Adam out of the seat. The bus driver yelled back to Adam, "If you cannot stay in your seat, you will not get to ride the bus tomorrow."

Adam knew the driver was serious because it happened a lot during the school year. The school called Adam's parents to discuss his bus behavior. They said it was a safety issue.

It was now when his parents decided to take Adam to see his doctor.

His parents figured a lot of Adam's behavior was because he liked sports and wanted to go outside to play soccer.

But Adam's older brothers didn't get into as much trouble as Adam did so they were getting concerned. Adam's dad, back in the day, would get into trouble, but they called it, "boy behavior".

Adam's doctor handed out forms to give to his teachers at school, his piano instructor, and his soccer coach. His parents were also asked to fill out the forms from their perspective.

The doctor needs the forms back by next week. He wants to see if Adam has similar problems in different environments. This information would help guide the doctor toward a diagnosis.

The doctor diagnosed Adam with ADHD or Attention Deficit Hyperactivity Disorder.

Adam's symptoms are an inability to sit still, blurting out answers, and daydreaming. The doctor reassured Adam and his parents that this was a treatable condition. He wanted Adam to see a behavioral therapist who could help Adam to become more aware of being in the moment.

He also suggested medication which he felt could help reduce Adam's symptoms. His doctor wanted Adam's school to know what was going on. He made suggestions to the school such as letting Adam take breaks and go for a drink at the water fountain.

That week, Adam started therapy. His therapist, Bob, started asking him when he noticed he would get into trouble the most.

Adam had no idea.

He knew that he was in trouble more than he wasn't. Sometimes it was for no reason, or at least that was how he felt.

Bob wanted to get started with an activity to help Adam.

Adam was to find 5 things in the office that had the color red in them.

First, he saw a red book on the bookshelf. The second thing he found was in a box of toys, a red Duplo piece. The third thing he found was the rug in the room had red lines in it.

As soon as he found the third item, he asked Bob if he could play with the metal plane he had displayed. Bob reminded him that he was still needing two more items.

This task was something he wanted him to do each day.

Bob gave Adam a printed list of things to find each day. The goal was Adam would write them out and have either his parents or a teacher sign off that he had found all 5 items.

Bob's hope was this exercise would help Adam stay in the moment and be able to follow through and finish the task. Adam would need to concentrate hard and not let his mind wander.

Adam started his medication. At first, he didn't notice a change.

What Adam did notice was that he was able to sit still in class. He was also less distracted by other kids, the birds outside, and the laughs from the hallway.

He caught himself remembering to raise his hand to answer a question instead of blurting it out.

Each week Adam met with Bob. He took the medication and noticed he was not getting in trouble as much.

While he still struggled sometimes, he felt happier that he was able to do better on tests and homework.

Adam sat on the bus in his own seat more so than in the past when he would jump up to sit with another friend. Adam knew that everyone wanted to see him succeed.

His parents, his teachers, the bus driver, and even his brothers all supported his goal. He was learning better ways to cope.

He realized some of the things he got in trouble for were not something he did on purpose. He had bad days too as we all do.

Today, as Adam sat in his college class, he realized that there was not a quick fix to his ADHD symptoms.

Medication wasn't a miracle drug. Therapy didn't make it go away. It was a combination of things.

He has a lot to do to manage himself, but he also feels like he is not alone and he has support when he needs it.

Resources

- Children and Adults with Attention Deficit Hyperactivity Disorder (CHADD)
  https://chadd.org

- Attention Deficit Disorder Association
  https://add.org

- The American Professional Society of ADHD and related disorders (APSARD)
  https://apsard.org

- ADDitude Magazine
  https://www.additudemag.com/additude-magazine/

- Understood
  https://www.understood.org/

- ADHD-Institute
  https://adhd-institute.com